Practitioner Joy

Practitioner Joy

RICH MURPHY

RESOURCE *Publications* · Eugene, Oregon

PRACTITIONER JOY

Resource Publications
An Imprint of Wipf and Stock Publishers
199 W. 8th Ave., Suite 3
Eugene, OR 97401

www.wipfandstock.com

PAPERBACK ISBN: 978-1-7252-6987-3
HARDCOVER ISBN: 978-1-7252-6986-6
EBOOK ISBN: 978-1-7252-6988-0

Manufactured in the U.S.A.   06/01/20

For Bonnie

The only truth is the inconsistent edifice of the logical
interconnection of all possible illusions.

—Slavoj Žižek

Modernity is the time in which those humans who hear the call to change
no longer know where they should start: with the world or with themselves—
or with both at once.

—Peter Sloterdijk

Contents

Acknowledgments

THANKS TO THE FOLLOWING journals.

Rumble Fish Quarterly: "Work Quirk" (nominated for Pushcart Prize 2019)

Former People: "Space Cadet" and "Morosis Diagnosis"

Otoliths: "Rainbow End"

Qutub Minar Review: "Microbe Morning with Caffeine"

Terror House Magazine: "Thought Controls," "Life-Long Learning,"
    "S. O. S.," "Terror Maintenance"

Poydras Review: "The Name Game"

The Transnational Magazine: "Straight Talk"

Former People: "Airbag Logos," "Todestrieb and the Parasite," and
    "Diurnal of Course"

West Texas Literary Review: "Inspiration / Expiration"

The Pangolin Review: "Drowning School"

Oddball Magazine: "The Lame Facts"

New Texas: "Ink Athletics"

Sein und Werden: "Ra Ra at Intergalactic Now U."

Futures Trading: "Birthplace Accidents"

From the Wound

Spirit is itself the wound it tries to heal, that is, the wound is self-inflicted. "Spirit" at its most elementary is the "wound" of nature.

—SLAVOJ ŽIŽEK

The most that any one of us can seem to do is to fashion something—
an object or ourselves—and drop it into the confusion,
make an offering of it, so to speak, to the life force.

—ERNEST BECKER

INSPIRATION / EXPIRATION

Poetry parents produce for door steps:
a practical joke in the neighborhood.

Wrapped in paper, a cry for help
written in bold print surprises,
and moms and dads pass
around the nursery rhyme time.

The pigpen playpen ends
after the clock pacifies,
and the thumb pinches with patience
at crayons, pencils, pens.

Elephant eared and needle-nosed,
the street-dwelling punch lines
steal from prose pros and blacken eyes.

In the street, a hand meets, shakes
due to itchy feet and insight
not commercial anxiety.

The awful orphan picks at solitude
caked on the sidewalks for future refugees.

With no room in a wallet for marriage
the lollygagger learns to straight-arm
the enthrall and cuddles at arm-length.

(Beneath mantles parading photos,
unwritten books burn in hearths
as soon as a match rubs for commitment.)

Only in old age does the social slouch
sleeping under a book tent wake to
affection afforded on the horizon,

a long night caressing the scalp,
the shoulders, the inner sigh.

RA RA AT INTERGALACTIC NOW U.

After the accident where instinct died,
road kill, and tradition, the first responder,
returned with an empty ambulance,
only species members with purpose
tucked into armpits hobble across anxiety
and boredom upon a rock in space.

The undriven limbs collapse among stones.
Passionate search parties turn over boulders
and knock down tall grass to find
fuel and mechanisms for livers lumped,
defeated consciousness, hardened hearts.

Uneven underfoot, the new day
that seems to break into momentary desires
begs for crutches and over-compensation.
Even lava, granite, and sand preach
at the school Beyond Expectation
where the best colleagues mine
personal potential for wellsprings.

Gripping the two railings, animal and angel,
at the No Hands Rehabilitation Center
everything rattles until from ancient holds
a questioner lets go to become.

THE PATRIOTIC FRONT

This is how he grows: by being defeated,
decisively, by constantly greater beings.

—Rainer Maria Rilke

The happiness go-getter tends
to the wound by donning a habit
until religious ritual stops the bleeding
and a daily routine forms scar tissue:
Boot camp bandage and drill passion
exercises so that kinesthetic replaces a flinch.

When the over-compensation ceremony
owns the peasant, the patient masters.

With needle-threaded possibility
the utopian practitioner stitches to gather
the brute face, indifference, (and a dopamine fix
gushes behind every dotted "i").

All other pursuits begin and end
with complicity between biology
and outsourced micro-/macro-managers.
Once embedded in desire the levers pry
and admen crowd at every fork carved
for the occasion, pushing beggar cups
in exchange for time and money.

The need nurse braces against want
with soup, bowl, and spoon.
After the chronic struggle to grow,
when on two feet outside the hospital,
a smile visits with no other gifts.

DANCING WITH THE STARS

More seductive than the Tango,
the dance "From Understanding
to Reason" turns on whole generations
with a new mirage to learn.

First, toes point out a critical step,
two and three and more delusions,
in the swing among once tumblers or tappers,
and then night reigns precipitating struggle.

Contortion troupes sell, foist, coerce, threaten
to express for all and forever the oncoming.
Does an angry public in the streets
salsa, cha-cha, merengue, mambo?

Eventually, everybody falls into rapture,
reorganizes and swoons into pirouettes
or leaps to become aerial acrobats.
With synchronized beating in whole gangs
the harmony brings forth the marching band
with birthing instruments and testing tubas.

A JIM BLUNDERS STORY

Wearing a party hat and carrying streamers
by the fistfuls, Jim Blunders
engages in routine daily.
Early in life "sit-up-straights"
and touchy toesies rest under the belt.

The rep representative lives
in New Hamster near an ol' treadmill
where aughta organs can't experience
the triage for the woulds
and memes for all eager beaver homo sapiens.

The Ta-Da dad stretches
into floor exercises and onto the expert tease.
Brushed and now polishing,
the noise-maker grunts and sighs
when performing without audience,
until flaws shape into wings.

Every practice session toward perfection
misses for the reveler, but with live people
in chairs in cheer even the critic peers
into a microscope to make note
while also dancing with the partner.
Whizzing past ears, rim shots punctuate.

THE RETICULAR ACTIVATING SYSTEM

At headquarters, the reticular activating system
draws on over-compensation practices,
particular tools, and materials
as the fleshed out skull crosses fields all day:
Psychology, biology, and ideology.

Ignored, the pro cons, high finance,
and unnecessary equipment fall aside.
The focus through primal trauma magnifies
until passion sparks and stampedes into a blaze.

Run-throughs challenge by greater expectations.
Concentration prepares for periphery filters
to sweep away more dross designed
by fetishes that lead almost always nowhere.

When interest clings to the memory magnet,
fire grows into animals fleeing to a call.
Every muscle and lobe brings to senses, so senses
bring to lobe and muscle magnificent failure.

TODESTRIEB AND THE PARASITE

Around the banquet tables at the cemetery
interest, lust, hunger quit
whether or not balmed daily earlier.

Strutting the latest designs from NASA
and sporting carnival bumpers, desire endures
beyond the havenly, folding body.

The tick-talking retirement party
lunges to catch up
with someone abandoned for forty years.

At the lounge for missing persons
golf club members beat with a driver
and chase with bourbon
to squander regret and redemption.

Stepping over the corpse, the pulp fiction
(a rung, a foothold) cries out an infancy
for which cultures scramble with wishes.

CONTESTANTS AT THE BAKERY

...reality has to be supplemented by fiction: to conceal its emptiness.
—Slavoj Žižek

Without host, consolation prize,
or parting gift, at birth the kitchen hand
kneads as needed or knuckles under,
all cheeks and flour on a table for a baker.

The fistful might learn to buckle
or curl into the creamier center,
a yogi meditating into nirvana
while a prep cook sprinkles and punches.
But death lacks no practice, no ingredient.

Having not asked for fingers and toes or knot,
most staller-and-bawler eyes in the queue
close to shill for an entire shrill.
Carnie thrill seekers and tumblers dare
to fill the air with motion sickness excitement.

Coaxing the shaggy batterer with palm heels
relieves for the battered and smoothes
into elastic the rules to ball anew
for no game show audience.

DIURNAL OF COURSE

Exact information of how to rearrange one's psyche in order to anticipate
the next blow from our own extended faculties.

—MARSHALL MCLUHAN

Earth-tumbling through illusions,
the critic reports where the seams
gather for stitching the seems series.

On the rolling spacecraft, knee-slapping
laughter substitutes for stabilizers.

In bubble wrap and connected
to the mother ship by an umbilical cord
vomiting tourists abound.

Astronauts without motion sickness
find in space what suits
and practice never looking back.

History hooks and star prongs
attend to god worshipers
allowing the acrobat to slip by.

The outerwear and inner care
for the big-top freak struggle
to bring better failures
to performance craft, too soon
dust debris forgotten around a sun.

TAG TEAM TUSSLE

"At present I would prefer not to be a little reasonable,"
was his mildly cadaverous reply.

—HERMAN MELVILLE

Though preferring not to,
the language lover leapt onto the rock wall,
wedging fingers into whorls below a brow
while feet found lip enough.

Face to face with the life sciences,
the Earth whisperer counters with rhetoric
that attempts to redirect or shape
the ideological breath heaved, threatening.

On the third stone from the sun,
the Atlas homunculus army wrestles
with the change in story-line that ends
with a period (a long one) for mutation.

The clay ball shape-shifts into a fungus
gob or amoeba blob to bury
the humanity fantasy slipping from hands
that seemed born to hold pens.

The humane phrase phase, where key terms
and active verbs spill from nibs
and dash from tongues, maneuvers
to negotiate reading room or parchment strip,

the left behind recording and commenting
"phew" to friends from the past.
Ears and eyes that made up the earth
embed in tombs, caves, an inside joke.

PARADIGM SHIP

Remnants and poisons from pleasure
pursuit experiments engulf
while the useless and hung-over scientist
collapses onto an overturned crate.

Curbing desire momentum
en masse threatens to fill streets
with violence technology.
Now, with default donut ideology
and using police when needed
governing elite push back
at logic and at consumer trash barrels
and dumpster overflow.

To turn the garbage barge
into a space ship with trimmed sails
and visible quarter deck, the hull
swill will empty spilling from three or four
Homo sapiens generations into a black hole.

All sextants retort at the pilot,
"no icebergs ahead."
Who talks to the crew?

AIRBAG LOGOS

Driving language all day and into the night,
insects punctuate for commas and periods
until the windshield wash and wipers turn on
and crafting sentences starts again.

Through dreams, the high beam headlights glare
at similitude and anxieties, one in the street
flattened and the other crossing in dark clothing.

The metaphor purring under the hood
gallops when a pen engages.
All likeness extensions on the road and off
appear to joy ride into the horizon,
but maps and purpose have been reviewed
by the wheelman (so-to-speak)
accelerating and braking.

Of course few pedestrians look at the streak
whizzing by when flipping pages
or at the black and white vehicle standing
at a podium with tongue wagging and arms flailing.

Poems may read at a glance,
but brains, backing up for photos
and deliberation in a back seat or sitting shotgun
while Smartphone buds beat with beat,
soon opt for the basic bounce that diverts traffic.

No, the writer with the-pedal-to-the-metal
or gingerly negotiating clutch and ledges
makes for tracks for the patient nursing
a new era or rambles to disturb dust,
one and the same practicing a utopia.

CAREER STEP SYSTEM

The attraction between gut guts
and cemetery worms choreographs
for each dopamine dodge
that forages in Frustration Forest.

Activating nimble sensors to perform
flawed routines while disregarding sit-coms,
attention-getting apps,
and bush-league PR campaigns
the dancer circles only to start again.

Practicing pirouettes or china-spinning
through the obstacle course, trips up
peak experiences and flow.
Dizzy bulls show up in living rooms
dreaming fame and fortune,
confusing personal with popular.

The prefrontal cortex tries to hide
brass rings and gold watches.

An amateur trail blazer tramps
until a morale compass stands up, a master.

THE LAME FACTS

The cries for crutches
flesh out new born acrobats.
Sidewalks on city streets,
difficult without obstacles,
bring on the high wire acts
along with the tumblers,
each overcoming a cripple.
With chests swelling out,
and with thanks to wounds,
the contortionists parade
to and from homes once a day.

No one celebrates from empty roads.

Only dogs, cats, and rodents,
who hock greater cerebral issues,
roam where the black and white
asphalt ribbon dares.

In either world, chains laugh
at the easy job predicament:
Restrain the already pained.
While lose couplings with feet up
meet missing links that wish
and leap, the lock to becoming
more picks via a pro.

JAZZ JOINTS

Without a socket for a hat,
the homo sapient head pivots
on the seal nose, Atlas/axis pinnacle,
alone grinding against stone
and a difficult place,
disjointed within solar system skin.
With flippers applauding the feat,
the balancing act pain suffered
by all species in the galaxy throbs.
On a wrist-watch, bone yards
also search for knee caps among ligaments.
Gauze pads and kisses cover infections.
Immune programs wear out
at humorus knobs, erogenous zones, and livers.
An anthropocene varmint unzipping
around the world opens up
the private parts to a deflating beach ball.
The self-conscious twist and shout (and then out)
beneath the jittery stars romanticizes
for narrative unity so that the dance
expresses hope among fragments.

ECSTATIC MAVERICK

The limbic system limbers up
moods and instincts that reach
for attitude then personality.
With little effort, a human hump
searches in the shell for an exit:
"Hello World." Meat happy to meet
while the selfless and psychopaths
wrestle in the schoolyard.

Ballet grace and yoga lotus yawn
grimace into second nature, striving for
a default drive neck and neck
with some chromosome character
that speeds from the spinal expressway.
Aroused neurons learn with time
long division in classes on a hippocampus:
Seahorse consciousness.

The mergers and acquisitions department
serve up the sting from busy B students
who won't forget about the As
and so zip from brain stem to body buddy.

Trip wires for the arrogant
and self assured stretch without safety nets.
The breeder beasts try to tip-toe
carrying open parasols.

VIRUS VIRTUE

Growing a chicken to make another egg,
a yolk jokes about a cock-a-doodle to do
(unless breakfast time in the farmhouse reckons
and then with sunny side up a sibling beckons).

The gizzard and feathered world dangles
on a thread for the embryo to bat around
should a predator miss an opportunity to wolf.

Would-be parents twiddle while waiting
for commands from a lustful soup chief
to mix the magic in the uterine caldron.

All the while the love simmers down
and doors kick flat from inside,
the kitchen help practices at uselessness.

The two D batteries, mom and pop,
charge, until depleted and tossed away,
through contact nipples and a dollar bill.
For headquarters, becoming
on Earth addresses within desire.

TUNNEL VISIONS

In the wind tunnel where graffiti warns
that only the cheater revives and revels,
tit-for-tat lovers exit through the light in eyes.
The fans whirl and cheer for evolution,
lifting the fair enough and stripping excess.

The cosmic flight may become for eternity.
Loyal prepositions and invented verbs
could tear from hands or from ducts.

The smartest pilots sit at lens grinders
holding wooden pencils with erasers on top,
capsules for the return journey.
Refining the kaleidoscope,
the viewer reveals again and again.

Life as a breeze whistles by,
debris seemingly designed to knock
the teeth from smiles.
But at the game table for skydivers
wingmen bet with wingmen.

LOADING DOC. (PH 7)

In an overheated evolution,
when steam billows
from the cooling system
and the lubricants
churn into asphalt,
the Mack Trucking and Company,
driven by Champ, the chimp,
pulls over to assess
and draw upon the expressway covered:

Monkey see, money do,
money do, money due.

The chump takes off the sheriff badge,
a cowboy hat, and climbs from the rig
to face up to the airbrake gasp,
to seven billion other bi-pedded lungs,
to species immunity decree efforts
flattened (road kill),
to the inevitable traipse
on common ground
by all legged creatures
that also leave no footprint no trace.

THE OVER-COMPENSATION GYM CLASS

While at the workshop for self-realization,
the leader exits at the start.
Eye-balls widen at each other until one-by-one
heads disappear into trial-and-error programs.

The room, cleared for various exercises
and activities, promotes from first
to last grades in eccentric natures
and graduation into madness.

First-breath wound remains for heaving
when the challenge slap arrives for jousting.
From then on, the red swollen cheeks
respond, engage, embrace.

The chandelier swingers and tackle dummies
along with virtuosos in screaming
and dance go about the businesses in excelling.

Meditator and mediator workout buddies
find in quiet, world peace.
Debate teams raise the roof and wrestle
over proper functions for bathroom fixtures.

The facilitator may return in a book
for statistics; the protégées oow and awe
at numbers but go to work training
through the big mime for the freak time.

Audiences and witnesses cheer or inspect
from along spectacle borders for possible
sidelines or transferable skills.

UNION NEGOTIATIONS

At the experience mediation session
expression acts out in the backseat,
free first and last. The child fidgets
after screaming "are we there yet?"

The seismic movements register
on paper filling for the moment
and then place on library shelves.

Feeling a way in the room available,
the eye-straining and ear training
strive for a place for a sense,
if not evidence for belonging.

Comfort food patches at best
while a taste for home muscles
against high fruit and low overhanging
ledges on the trail to who-knows-where.

Squiggling and scribbling don't hold up
in museums or books but rob
for the moment the effort for life:
"The intimacy insulted as . . ."

Happening goes on and on
when dirt stands in for a writer.
Without resolution except
for the one-sided agreement:
Cymbals crash and crash and crash . . .

THE HEIGHTS IN THE PRISON YARD

Sentenced to life imprisonment
with high labor, the language stunts read taut.
Craning necks up to focus on a thin line,
the reader trains to become wire
or the long balancing pole in hands
or to possess step by step the feet
that forgo the rhyme, a net-less feat.

In the clouds without an umbrella
a chain gang member wobbles
on the tightrope to fix eyes steady.

The point always mist upon the crowd
on the rock pile below and upon the cheeks
holding an inner ear for words.

The rhythm for the soles that dance
about subject and about object
and for the iris twins in concentration
while following a lead across a chasm.

The team Thrill Seekers and Friends
teem in the moment, in "Hurray!"

WADING INTO THE CITY

Should the poet stand in culture
wearing hip boots, fortunate feet
plant but passion stinks along
with the birth and death all around.

No Petri dish-walled experiment.
Welcome to free-range fauna and flora
where Homo sapiens birth defect
pretends at amateur hour.

Reptilian slime mucks up the dry humor,
a wetland field day everyday
so to speak in a croak, perhaps.

Without patience for the painting,
architecture, or poem to fix psyches
lame naturalists concoct to affix lenses.

Still, the foul bog bubbles up metaphors
and miasmic images from below:
pheromone and rot = methane et al.

So an artist rinses in a genome before
dipping into social stagnation colors
to slap awake the viewers.

The environmental designer draws on
raw materials to surround
with an engineered virus watch.

A writer pokes at the keys nuanced
for lobe globes that focus black on white.

"PARADE" ROUT

No meaning-meat rewards inside nouns
and verbs that spill out over casks
with bottomless diaphragms
from every corner on the planet.
The diplomatic theaters around the world
close in the evening so that poets
sweep up the littered word-shells.

The silence smith, who once knew
how to rhyme scheme, disposes for a town,
satisfies with the podcasts.
Muffled sounds remain for crafting,
(emoji, cliché, bytes) misshapen casings
with a gunpowder smell.
Using any container available,
barges, dumpsters, carpet caverns,
the husk hauler presses into service.

Happy to sigh, the bard with a broom
stoops with relief and a whist pan
though every breath anticipates
live ammo, not fireworks, not chatter.

Letter-filled thought-balloons pass for verse.
Dirigibles dialogue and dream in the skies,
but only the thoughtful look up
while impulse faith in emotion triggers.
The Sunday funnies once saved for a day.

THOUGHT CONTROLS

The friction and flooding information
sensors calibrate for readers:
The industry-produced bliss current
and thinkers don't mix.

Deluges dilute until stream-resistance
surveillance dumps in the abrasives,
time and money, to wear down fact checker,
dot connector, and imagination initiator.

Called in only for emergencies, e-engineers
experiment in sandboxes, on rock piles,
and with dog muzzles, while measuring for affect.

Too busy commuting with cliché
and platitude, the debtor and dance partner
exhaust until rabbit holes riddle the day.

Whole nations sleepwalk into tomorrow
owing breath to singers channeling television.
Two shackles each and motivational GIFs
chew on literature, peruse until geniuses
begin springing up all over.

MOUNT IMPROBABLE

Plain terrain, having stacked plates
after dinner for Gaia and humped stone
for Sisyphus, then looked to springs
and spring for self improvement.
Bald, arch-browed and, halfway down,
a rumpled tree line, a reflective peek
quakes beneath 10,000 feet above the sea.

Disheveled and wrinkled—though few rappel
from the face or fear the switchbacks.
Crowded with day-hikers on a ridge
and family campers on a ledge,
the trophy shelves weigh on slopes
for distinction to mark the planet.

Mountain ranges tower all around
the late rescuer summiting with an image
on a lake surface, questioning ravines:
The unlikely elevation taps at the sky
for an opening, a way to grow in stature.

FOSSIL FUSELAGE

In the Goldie Locks Zone Time Capsule
an enlightenment shone on Mt. Improbable,
where from depths consciousness streams
bubbled up here and there and, babbling,
quenched for thought.
In the notion ocean, the swishes, wishes,
and fishes posed for questions.

The scientist and entrepreneur poked
and prodded from a boat for answers and cash
during the interview process.
Exhausted cars pile up and promise
to early bone yard futures batched
and boxed people stacked on city shelves.

All the while, on a visionary launch pad,
space craft inches into neighborhood interiors
from shorelines: A sustainable home
for lions, tigers, and humans.
Poets and tiny inheritors sing
for an opportunity to dance tomorrow.

Will the elbow room increase enough
for arm-in-arm for kicks and deliberation?

_____

(One word or fewer)

BROKEN RECORDS

Juggler, gymnast, meditator
line up for the Nietzsche Practice Prizes
in categories object, body, mind.
No fans, no audience, no opponent,
records from previous years whip up
the stiff competition who then salve
selves on gurneys on the sidelines.

Each club, each pommel horse,
each empty mind rehearsed
by a lone on-looker misses out
on performed perfection
but edges toward death and the forgotten.
Yet the acts that challenge tomorrow
delight with the rite stuff.

The stage, stage, stage for best habits
applauded by thunder . . . perhaps,
flashes with the spotlight on ceremony
that pulls the symbolic from an animal.

WHAT WISHED FOR

Occupied by Daedalus pregnant with Icarus
particles and waves, the Birthing Institute
for greasy bio-mechanics jiu-jitsus the Renaissance
to arrive on Mount Olympus: Hera or Zeus anyone?
Even Voltaire would fall for the frontal-lapel-
shoulder-throw coming full on –
El Greco may be pleased when teased.

Silicon may strut as though Achilles
on a beach while a guy with the wrenched back
taking orders, obeying and while some heckler
hectors on the walls ends up a drag king
and all Helen has broken loose.
But then what about the archway, the heel?
The archer monkeying with string and bough
may aim to become: better than waxing forecasts.

BIVOUACKING WITH BIG BOYS

At the base camp for Mount Ikigai
most climbing parties practice
on the plateau day and night
and dream around planted flags.
The legs up the wall and face plan out
well at the fire pit cramp therapy sessions.

Distractions blister on simulators
in the great outdoors when traction cleats
cheat for cartwheeler and tumbler floor routines.
Excuses blossom next to the tents
where logo-gnats brand professional gear.

Sherpa guides and alpine mountaineers
make up the summit expedition.
Boots and praxis wear at slopes
where balance beamers and scars
competitors wear for the children within.

SCHOOLYARD RECESSES

Trapped within adults, the children
running around spinal cords
thump on walls inside livers,
cry out in mammoth chest caves,
and kick at the lobes
that orchestrate behavior.

The tikes let out from the come-on
instinct stallions and genome grizzlies
whenever possible.
Teens pass in judgments to parents
who fake lessons learned
and seldom make the grade.
State leaders suck on thumbs
when alone in hotels and in bedrooms.

The hell raised rampages
from within double-helix stair wells
and points out scapegoats,
plots against friends,
and passes for love,
as though justice shows up
on the streets nearby.
If practicing cooperation for centuries
ever embeds in chromosome chains,
even the dog would benefit.

THE SELF-POSSESSION SPLASH

Becoming in the Routine River,
where swimming carries a passion,
lessons begin when an observer
on a bank enters the water.

Learning the difference between
a stone and a fish . . . and a fish
from a container for desire,
the surface slapper and kicker grows.

Habit circles around with ripples
until the challenge wakes with ache
and the shore for no thanks waves
goodbye and the sure for a self
tests for clarity in the change.

Each addition and subtraction
that brings about a second nature
exhales where the shallows haunt
with weaker and weaker impulse.

When the banks catch breaths
for gasping loungers and students,
the Olympian bold mettler,
who long ago lost meddler for a name,
shows off acorns and a new trick.

The bow with a smile after
the performance gestures to the tree
limb balcony bumblers and well
wishers: Well come . . . to practice.

STRAIGHT TALK

What mother tongue articulates,
listeners define until every detail matters.
Bouncing on the taste-budded tip,
the apprentice warms up and down
before the dive for practice into judgment.
Around the globe, the language
and mood jump for the possible master
(who with a smirk sits in the audience
elbowing a neighbor to left and right.)

Children fall and routine dresses
for survival: loose tops for bones
and blousy bottoms for muscles –
and on special occasions tights with glitter
to inspire pops in heaven.

Wimple over a dimple!
Good habits fit; rabbits rhyme.

Should a full-throated journeyman
trudge across that training stage,
a blue ribbon pins to a shoulder
an authentic attitude
but not to smooth sailing.

Even during death rehearsal, a smile slaps
around the amateurs in the waiting room:
Who can tell whether Wrinkles
cracks up during the leg-pulling?

Perfection doesn't call, doesn't write;
found nowhere. Only rumor whispers
something about excellence,
and so every poem says, "again."

POEM SUITE POEM

Building roofs first, poets bite at nails
when hammering home to hold
and when constructing a village for tourists:
Quick, quick! No, straight lines for once;
measure twice and cut once, and so forth.
Late within the eves, the planted
typewriter blooms to heavenly bodies.

Stories or floors come together in feet,
tongue and groove with shine,
and four walls at a time that may rhyme
or not but studded and bearing the load
while windows open and perhaps one
with some saw hanging from the valance.

Even the shingle painting feathers in
landscaping brush and bush
so that the poured concrete language
finishes for the poem about homes
challenging rodents and rot upon entering.
A reader may move in for free if desired,
but the neighborhood and community
musical chairs inspires ongoing outings.
Driving a last tacky point: From the top!

DROWNING SCHOOL

Each drip and drop
from the information fire hose
at hand in a palm colors
from navel to headstone
in a world calling for decisions.

At the nozzle, the incredulity filter
without default fluctuates
between open and shut off only.

A human nature in firefighter garb
responding to roaring and squeaking
gurgles among stained-glass
momentary beliefs and resolution.

The life-vest that buoyed a heart sinks
beneath the worry stone rock-slide.

From the mound beside mountains
Regret and Misunderstanding,
where tree and beast suffer at hands,
a spent potential rests on habit still.

Cheerleading Squad

[I]t is only one step from the existentialism
of the handicapped to that of acrobats.

—Peter Sloterdijk

CYCLING AROUND THE WORLD

With mixed feelings on planet Identical
girls and mothers squeeze from uteri
herd thinners and scapegoats.

Doctors at the scene refuse to use
label guns on Homo sapiens
entering the great outdoors.
So clone siblings with arms
grow from arms to arms.

Discovered when a spotlight shines,
flaws appear in the space craft
management system operations.

Because paranoia inoculates all toddlers,
years pass before the difference
between clubs and a club dawns
on victims who wish to own slaves:
Group hugs that happened behind
closed doors in the dark shrink in size.

But ignorance wags and licks at
the hunter who heels every morning
until terror one at a time
cleans clocks in old age.

S. O. S.

The leaky denial system sinks
into death terror-sweats,
into the desire fire in the body,
and into experience/language impossibility
unless family, friends, neighbors bail.

Bucket brigades from port to starboard,
fore and aft strain to smile
while dumping overboard anxiety and fear
into the deep blue despair tides:)
"Have a good day" insists!
Words and business-at-hand hold
for the hull where neurosis wears
four gold stripes on an epaulet
with anchor insignia and bell bottoms.

Admission squirts and gushes
from holes into hold along the draft
and below the water line and sick bay.
The ballast tank loses balance at birth.
To keep from seaing, boys and the gullible
bob and gasp in the harbor gale.
The salt stings when in the wounds.

"Once upon a time . . ."
and "happily ever after . . ."
the corks that plug, function to save
the drowning victim when strung and sung.

BAD HAIR DAYS

From infancy to heckler or to rock thrower,
"worse," the grooming system for the rabble
differs in the method but not intent.

A father might comb through a psyche
with tools from a wood shed after a hammer
replaced a dream decades ago.

A belly could share with mom
peas from a can again and again
long after the bread winner left.

A voyeur may observe for 20 years
where parents hurt (without a mumble)
more and more without available care.

Though biology and chemistry
mix up a concoction at a keyboard also,
the meticulous face for change readies
for footing and for grip before
the practical joke, punch line response.

FIRST RESPONDERS

The scar tissue that throbs in dreams
sometimes escapes even from the ribcage
and acts upon the world at large, a bird at prey.
A field mouse or cat disappears,
a fellow human may writhe and droop,
unless daylight cuffs the talons.

The misfortune that pumps blood perches
upon organs, muscles, bones
to scab over until denial sets in.

A city teems with pain while caffeine
highs apply a hit-or-miss salve.
Should the wounds tunnel out
or callus over to distract the flesh
that binds, bandages, teeth and nails
expose for voyeur headlines
in *The Mirror Daily*: a fact
to embarrass the mob in uniform
always posing for the history book.

IMPOSSIBLE MOUNTAIN

The Absolute species, fragile in nature,
as with other members from the erect Identicals
families, continue to climb Mount Improbable.
Neanderthal grandparents would faint
from the thin air on the altitudinal tundra.

At the tree line the look-alikes in glass houses
so inclined to peek experiences venture outdoors.
Some sure-footed bi-peds
trail-blaze to higher terrain –
saddle, spur, ridge, and threatening snowy cap –
while others decline the risk to practicing talent.

An attentive shepherd listens
for the buzzing to being
to heed bleating dreams and efforts
and to take in what rose to blossom so far:
No bluff where tectonic plates
under a meadow separated from wolves
from sheep enough to persist in becoming.

THE SACRIFICE

Scaring crows perhaps, fantasies
and ideas dig in against existence,
but graveyards boot-print the Earth
several times over: Bones at home.
Tomorrow and the next day promise
for trenches and daisies in mutation.

Behind front lines, behind insurance
company and investment bank totem towers
the mechanical and addicted actors
take cover from accidental bruising.

Unable to believe in the rites and laws
that guarantee decades for manicured lawns
and annual physicals, the motion threader
bubble-wraps plans in order to stay executions.

The straight-faced comedian vaults
over the cheapest thrills under the sun
to avoid the audience dying
from laughter just beneath flesh.

CANNED GOODS

Eating self-esteem from a can,
the need to fill a hole gnaws
when multimedia pave over
farms and gardens with confetti
to starve couch potatoes
and any body sprouting a spirit.

Fresh fruits and vegetables deliver
daily for free to bankers, silent
partner scientists, celebrities,
and the hero manufacturers
who parade about with chests out.

Designed to encourage envy
and discourage empathy,
the long-resigned learned helplessness
practices and the strutting deservers,
embedded in the mud for impulse only
epoch upon epoch upon epoch.

At the nipple for planetary homelessness,
the recent refugee, also on the border
to second nature, looks back ashamed,
embarrassed to have been a member.

TERROR MAINTENANCE

Names change but the in-house
inferiors inventory remains.
At the ends of each day,
the alphabetical order sags with labels,
dog whistles, and euphemisms.
Warehouse management
and stock control foremen determine
when to leave barn doors ajar
and when to declare open season
on bottom-shelved people.

Out-sourced hate only goes so far.
The obvious primitive tribes
and backward venturing dolts
in the wilderness tire out
the armed missionaries
in all-terrain vehicles.

Reflection and assessing within
rout out the lazy tales
and short cuts in the party line.
If not comparison, then the story
that the mob memorized and narrates
all day and night judges for value.
No antidote anecdotes win with laughter
or a declarative brief death sentence.

GHOST STORIES

A thousand eyes hang fixed from a wall
and from a poem stare back at a viewer.
Few humans from the invited engage
in conversation or in a staring contest.

Monologues from canvas stretchers
or page sheets seem to threaten
when audience members stand
in foyers in galleries or libraries.

More apt to lash out with insult
than with questions for relation;
visitors rush by park benches
or tear up dirt roads with four-wheel drive.

Ghosts from earlier generations look on
for embrace from the embedded within in-kind
framework now embarrassed and homeless
unable to invoke family codes for entry.

THE UNDERGROUND

Imagined and engineered,
poems bore through
the manuscript pages
so that other language trains
for thought may pass on the way,
once again, to distraction.

City and town crowd out
with elbows and gossip
dangling and glittering before eyes.
Numbing until paralyzed
to avoid death inklings,
the screen surfer drowns
for a day, each day.

To catch breath and more
to practice possibility
with becoming-aid and advice,
sore rib cages and lied-to chumps
exit into the catacomb
meditation gyms, the subway
recharge stations for the spirit.

Demise-denying delusions
turn inside out to live art
on the street and in homes
when morning coffee opens eyes
to frailty and toasters pour
a flute to the silence in tombs.

STANDING OVATION

At the Heroism Theater,
where, without exits,
victims take turns pretending;
if the mask lifts a fan base,
death shrinks for a mob
that then attacks a scapegoat.

The cycle thins out actors
and audience faster than old age
though generations replenish
with stunt men and talented women.

Since stage and house lighting crews,
schools for rehearsing tea
with denouement, for practicing
the bow before the curtain drop,
holiday to celebrate money and power
while memorizing breaths in and out.

To calm the winds in drama
and to weaken the villain approaching,
the joke-by-any-other-name
chuckles early and greets
with expectation an old friend.

SIR FACE

Serfs up for waxing boredom
so that paddling out to a "swell"
reply drowns out the person
trapped in debt labor for life.

A hello wave crests goodbye
for the skimmer skipping along,
(a stone?) as though desire
for deep drafts has ebbed.

A body suffers in bondage
across the fields, factory floors,
and service industry on the manor.
The surface tool self-adjusts soon
after hired to fix discomfort for a lord.

The shallow engagement
through breathing, where a heart beat
for the mannered owner
pumps crafted on a sleeve,
the Homo sapiens in skivvies begging
weighs for a waiter and librarian alike.

DESTINATION TREPIDATION

Shivering while imagining peak
experiences, people huddle
in the valleys to form audiences.
The snow caps that exercise bring
to aptness chills from brain stem
to tailbone while membering applauds.

Most potential climbers with gear
and energy learned how to fear
the insects, animals, switchbacks
and coming face-to-face
with sheer rock and open sky.

Opting for the couch crouch
at the foot for dream-following,
the vicarious victors practice
at labeling evidence for bench warming
though the habit, current until uphill
flow-zone, risks little against life-support.

With a knack packed on the back,
an anxiety transformer stowed in the ribcage,
repeatable legs below (step one, step two),
and a pathway sprinkled with sunny days,
the wrinkled brow glimpses at a threatening
brow and waits for the occasional wink
before leaping to the talent trek.

HOUSE PAINTER

Too long rested against the wrong wall
the ladder to success taunts.
On the lower rungs for thirty years
the daunted climber resents
when another morning points out
the height and cost in the mirror.
The step-round imprinted on dreams
for furniture and a mortgage.

The money needed to appear
as a member on the sidewalk and loved
by family and friends siphoned off
five or six days each week.
The flow pooled in impulses
that drowned a human in amnesia:
Any reflection flashed just before
nursing home dementia and drivel.

A crash course for death so that senses
awaken redirected into cubical gardens
and computer streams, both as though natural.
Aligning body with one desire for life
corkscrewed into distraction:
Coulda, shoulda slaps at a ranch house
and sponges down a Mustang.

BIRTHPLACE ACCIDENTS

Born with a sash weighted by merit badges,
Fauntleroy tips over in playgrounds
and nods off in front rows during class times
after pulling blue ribbons to the chin.

Schooled in place-holding from birth,
the extra-curricular bellies roar with hunger
when cramming in an education for the last resort:
Each proof an equation, "losers grow into losers."

The good scout cliché looks out for number one
and the bottom line for the trophies to win,
while the poor lout uses night vision goggles
in a foreign land that harbors natural resources.

The American knows from the start that the drill
divides into two: One plus none on flash cards.
Justice rationalizes so that resentment dies early
in bodies, voice, or energy = a bowled over score.

An immigrant with a spangled attention span
pledges to act out scapegoat along with neighbors.

THE TALENT CONTEST

When free private lessons
in thumb-twiddling
schools to learn helplessness
and a whole underworld program
for killing time dangle before a nose,
deciding which, if any, among
three silver spoons feed
racks for torture.

The talented gum chewer
leans against the laurel tree
when drawing straws.
Though the sore thumb gift
throbs for ongoing attention
from overcompensation,
time for examining quality
ladles and utensils abounds
without hot soup or deep difficulties.

Putting off the practice and failure
outside game, the inner domain
risks and atrophies so that the old knack,
finesse, and aptness substitute
for a sought novelty day-in and day-out.

LIFE-LONG LEARNING

The exits leak but bolt to deliver
attendance at the Anxiety School.
Clocks peal at learners for attention.
An apple peels at eye lids.
Only the student pleas.
Around every quad corner
change threatens with death.
Can the math genius figure out?
Can the language whiz decipher?
While small stakes play out
the melodrama for classroom and class
from the core, terror eats and squirms
through to the pupil in eyeballs,
to lips, to finger tips.
Lab rodents train for crawling
over the dead bodies.
Every passive moment still,
every hand thrust into the air,
every jog to memory and back . . .
Worn by fear, denial stretches
from the foot to the scalp.
The Homo sapiens stiffens
from a primal sneeze to the coffin.

WORK QUIRK

Something to say rampages
through the cranium.

Bushmen shinny up the brainstem.
Temples rumble with china shop revelation.
A voice box mashes into finger tips
while tectonic plates sound out
and shape for the décor and the elephant.

When eyes sizzle with broken dawn,
a secretary for a state
heads for the round table.

Navigating the unscaled,
the note taker for trunk and task soothes
where wrinkles on clef paper challenge.

A stenographer in climbing shoes
interprets for an independent mind.

Passion rattles in the percussion section
while an engraver attends to observe
and to recommend to the wind
instrument and keyboard.

Negotiating to strike deals
between experience and "thud,"
takes in time and gives back change.

So metaphor police rely on a forger
always returning to the scheme
to move heaven toward earth.

The gray day seams with silver lining
as long as the misunderstanding
results in wallpaper.

MICROBE MORNING WITH CAFFEINE

On a good day, biological storms
form within the Homo sapiens interior
where high pressures and low compete
for enzymes and where the go-zone
layers to preserve the precariat
and subsistence wagers.
Short-term convenience-climate-makers
smooth out acid reigning in bellies,
using cup holders, fast food, and blue tooth.
The cranium absorbs for the mistaken
heart, the bad blood.
Ignoring organ monsoons, muscle twisters,
nerve and brain hurricanes,
the smile feigns for friendship
and for hidden knife-fight waltz:
Wind, rain huff and seldom bluff.
Destructive paths trail blaze
from Achilles heel through fatty tissue
and ligament to the crown frown,
drowning livers, triggering internal combustion
chambers, and gutting frontal cortexes.
Under a microscope diabetes chews on wallets.
The barometric anemia falls jaundiced
into a terminal cumulus syndrome.

INVERSION THERAPY

Siphoning excess sexual energy
from glands and organs, the brainstem
stores and converts for habit.
The rite stuff or routine hunger
for fuel to sculpt the sculptor
from childhood beyond the lot
planned by family, friends,
neighborhood, city, and fate.
Passion directs from the overstuffed
spleen, the blah, blah to Cipherville
unless a lens brings to focus.
Tantrums and orgasm laugh at
a fool who chased through nerve
for the spectacle to brag about maybe.
Funnel the fuel through praxis
and fail until the hand holding
a tempered steel blade controls,
and the rock block becomes.
Once alive, the metamorphosis
engages in conversation through work
and little by little transforms
the coarse riffler helper.
At this point in the chipping,
the audience eavesdrops for fragments.
The making-for-life flashes
and runs off any cliff or pedestal
with an aligned hurrah for breath
by the self-chiseler, Nick, in promotion.

RATIONING RATIONALE

Wringing panic into reason
for paralysis, worry stones
or rosary beads busy until fear
and hunger disguise weapons as tools.
En masse each hero system digests
for teeth that greet with a smile.
Diplomats, armies, and bank rolls
negotiate along the borders.
Coming face to face that size-up
during cultural niceties,
mouths open to compare
until the bigger gullet swallows.
The surviving intestine
with intact palate writes for historians
that the great god ladles out goods
and defines the good.
Made from glass and steel
the totems match taboos for luck.
Meteor or flood may lurk,
but the prescient preyer
guffaws at second nature.

RAINBOW END

In the democratic desert,
where the lesser evil drifts
when the wind storm howls,
the Bedouins walk until bones
can't cast shadows.

Ownership shifts, sifts into mirage.
Watery selves bubble up from pores.
The sun and sand collude
to bake flesh loaves for vultures.

Green voices skirt the doom,
and tribal areas wait
for drumming fingers
to fill the streets without a hero.

The dream, to dilute fear
into solutions, to quench thirst
for scapegoats with dialogue,
to soak impulse with second nature,
perches, a pigeon, on tongue tips.

EPIC RUB 21ST CENTURY

When fictions friction and burst into flames,
the boy scouts haven't arrived (and won't)
with marshmallows, chocolate, and kumbaya,
but pointy sticks weaponize in a pinch.

The old and the new tall tales grumble
and roar at the abutment, but tellers
and believers populate within the train
for history and cultures: Wooing (and chewing).

Should an edgy generation fall
through the crack that divides,
streets fill with placards and punches,
guts and guns, and ground bodies between.

Rival rivers run against each other:
Some flee, some chase, and some butt
to confront with adrenalin coursing
red through the rocky ravine.

No end in sight for the friction fiction
until no ends at the site, only epochs
interlocking in imaginations:
Hands shake until handshakes in legends.

Always in medias res, Colossus straddles.

CAREER PATHS

Fanning out across the fields,
– biology, sociology, history, etc. –
peasants search for recognition.
The shrubs and tall grasses obstruct,
preventing clear vision, and no gatherer
plans to find a dead body.

Filling silos with trivial data,
the seekers mark for the lords
at the manor who issue merit badges
in the hard candy wrappers
that twist at both ends.

Golden handcuffs fit into fewer
and fewer trophy cases.
Instead, a clerk rubber stamps
certain documents "expert"
and the bonus forager
turns to cipher in computers.

Laurels rot in barns and warehouses,
while croppers add to score cards
and wait on awarding eyes to raise
a salary or office prestige.
Each member in the search party
never dreams to self-congratulate,
or mumble "what else in this world?"

ATLAS ROLLING AROUND

Somersaulting without mats
through history a generation
may start on two feet
but end on backs, humiliated,
or head tucked squatting in fear.
Many spines snap upon landing.
Every return to soles
interjects with amnesia.
The floor routine gymnasts
slime with destruction in wake:
army slugs slog across a coliseum,
momentum gone to crutches.
No cart, no wheels either.
Animals fly into extinction
from the site and pound
or settle for slave contribution.
The tumbling practice perfects
for self-annihilation
the dizzy prophets say.
Perhaps one-by-one an idea
can peel at the Sapiens Ball,
where predator feigns genteel,
so that walking or standing
in thought trends for the way.

DEATH DRIVE SALES DEPARTMENT

Down-time at the International Praxis Center
demonstrates for the practice initiate.
Passions up-end corral desks, flip over
gym mats for talent left behind a day ago.

The impulsive liver drowns in another addiction.

The limbic limberer watches for word choice,
reads for behavior, turns inside out motives
and outcomes, especially the unintended.
Inscape exposes to help the suspicious doer
with insightful expeditions to death
when the homage baton passes on.

Recovering from a strenuous foreign week-eater
or bad whether decisions that have the imagination
stretch this way and that and running up staircases,
headquarters for routine learns from experience.

The meme person takes on the mean player within
at the Coliseum for History and Tomorrow
where average hangs and rots from flow charts.

MOOD MOVER

No one wanted Mike Mulligan and Mary Anne anymore.

—Virginia Lee Burton

Brimming with anger and isolation
until filled with sadness and solitude,
each morning the steam shovel
idles under a shower and then
reaches out an arm with a bucket.

The excavator, following an Arc Angel
across the sky, dumps into the hole
that hungers with need each day:
Antinomies antagonize to model meaning.

Unloading an alphabet into a trench
until the letters blurt out a good night
above and around, the heavy machinery
repeats for poetic justice all week.

The deep desire for Parnassus
to own no slope, no slouch
and only shoulders for carrying higher,
fuels with metaphor and irony
so that the backhoe smiles now and again.

The Return with Exit Signs

The philosopher knows about this from his own existence, for he has
discovered the cave's exit . . .
If he simply remained enlightened on his own behalf, he could bask in his
private happiness; if he is seized by concern for the state, however, he must
abandon privatism and seek to share illumination with the many.

—Peter Sloterdijk

SHELF LIFE

Unlike beasts, the shelf-conscious
human stores and displays.
Canned goods stack past sell-by date
and trophies oow & aah at the dust
raining upon what shines.

The shelfish goon lugs upon shoulders
and piles on tables, arm rests, stools,
hassocks, cupboards, and furniture
ledge lips for easy access.

Framed photos, television remote,
newspapers, computer mouse,
propped photos, and a dictionary
weigh on the stained book case.

The gazelle carcass on the savanna floor
and the antler racks moving along
the forest walls prod the hoarder.
Saved for later, lessons accumulate
with fat for emergency rooms.

Any selfless mantel haunts with nooks,
and grannies nail down lace curtains.

Crouched on a couch for all eyes to price,
the prize possession waivers
between potato and packrat,
while envying the Spartan, the shellfish.

OR BUST

After naming personal low spirits
and identifying woe mentors from the blahs
among the living-dead, the walker
in the valley for unrecognized despair exits
to climb Mount Improbable alone.
The camper packs for carrying survival on the back:
Canned talent and mess kit, tuck-away habits
with expandable purpose poles, and a canteen
filled with passion. All easily accessible.

The anonymous hiker becomes
and becomers everywhere note that the newcomer
has need for the unseen helpers.
Hands from under rocks, maps showing
forest for trees, and a sunlit door opens ahead.
In lookout towers earlier becomers watch
for devotion following up a childhood gift:
A bowling pin, a top hat takes on a center stage.

Jugglers and magicians practice for performance
and extract from eyes: "WOW!"
Never arriving on Ikigai Peak, the unarmed
violinist thanks at the Desire & Meaning Junction
for the many rolling mounds around Parnassus.

SECRET AGENT

I have the feeling that my books get written through me
and once they have got across me I feel empty and nothing is left.

—CLAUDE LEVI-STRAUSS

The crossroads watch for commuting ideas,
reckless words driving alone
and trailer truck assertion insertion
with a horn blaring on the way by.

A bald metaphor swooping at this,
sweeping at that along an expressway
aspires, ruffles to alert feathers, and flies on.
The eye-witness who drummed
on a keyboard, now dances.

After a particular brush on a shoulder,
after passing lanes and the stop lights,
and after the report on traffic,
hitch-hikers, and the state police,
days pass before the interchange arrives
again alert on the scene.

FOUR-WAY YIELD

...something happens here.

—CLAUDE LEVI-STRAUSS

By the time the school bus arrives
at the crossroads rusted,
the actors had gathered with tents
to roast the sausage
in the breakdown lane.

The expert butchers had already gone
to work on location from butt-cheeks
to masks to finger tips
performing the antagonists
in " The Struggle," a drama without play.

Fed up until stuffed outside-in
with every muscle, ligament,
and fat tissue, the gastro-testament
declared that from lips to gut to sphincter,
"Raw, raw, raw."

"Hot Dog!" shouted out some cool kid
wearing a bell around the neck
and a baseball cap.

When the laughter got roaring
enough, the grill ignited.
Skewered and fun-poked
until any star in the night eyes
mirrored human, the giggle sizzle winked,
and the link without a wiggle
or flop left for the worms.

HOMO SAPIENS PROTOCOL

The psyche surgeon hunts
for emotional short-comings
and ignorance hidden
behind feigned confidence.

But first, wearing a headlamp,
the miner, armed with rolled sleeves
and a sharp brass instrument,
peels away colonies, impresses,
and biases: The parasites
that drain time and energy.

Reaching beyond immediate
pleasure principals, cornets
announce when from humiliation,
shame, and terror primal desire crowns
a second birth, a be-knighted royalty.

The womb wound inflicts to prod practice,
the praxis package that never ends.

A high chair from which to direct,
act, and edit waits
for the over-compensation master
to arrive from the audience
to surprise a species worthy.

THE NAME GAME

Personal identity rubbed off
along uterine walls perhaps.
Fellow hollows: Hello,
Hell . . . o, hhh.
Look into the mirror all day,
pinch at forearm flesh,
poke at ghosts donning
foot and head wear: No one there.
The license photo, the passport
number lead to black holes.

An owl under a dunce cap parrots.
The hippocampus hunts
for a National Geographic photographer
to register survival techniques.
The label gun practices on canned goods
but misses with every shot:
On sale for $0.00 with or without coupon.

A stick man in a field for study
puts on a uniform that never launders
so that at least a crowd waves.

Bulls-eye nipples at the crossroads
wound with expectation.
Lips and larynx make up the rest.

ILL WILL AND THE FURNACES

1

During the success phase
for the immune system
when pulmonary heaving operates
to feed the cardiovascular pump,
the bio-chemist rummages
through the natural world
to study low hanging fruit,
roots, and pre-fixes to compounds.
The automaton in a lab coat
erases for the present moment.
Without control, the cyborg
creates for celebration
beyond epidemic, beyond human:
Algorithm defending a logic.

2

Hoping to find chests in an attic,
feet with vision on a page,
the philosopher swears upon trends
in techno-capitalism that contingency
may bubble up into eyes.
An option for the flesh and honed
dweller may be to wave for the last
to the numbed nose-cone
belonging to an empathy illusion.

3

The city citizens, hides
covering survival skill sets,
hide beneath flower
and four-poster beds.
The burning class in sleepwear,
suffering from the energetic imperative,
feels around for the immediate surroundings
to identify a thought.
Missing the point that jabbed
for planting through patient practice,
the desire fires invest in a future
not wanted or needed.

UTOPIAN FRUITS

Shepherding inner concerns out
(each bundled fear and desire),
the staff and horn from yesterday
triage through the confusion
from waking moment to fastening
bells onto valued instinctual
and colonized consciousness.

Fitbit, smartphone, laptop
impress with form and content
as a simple hunger bleats for rescue
from the brambles but pleads
to sacrifice comfort to the wolves.

A woolly meadow red with entrails,
knoll grasses no more for lounging in,
a knell buries in an abandoned churchyard
(would have been, would have been)
and the ushering forth continues.

The ad hoc procession with entourage
emerges through eyes for other trained
contingency adapters also enacting
for new heights on an indifferent planet.

MOROSIS DIAGNOSIS

Returning to homeostasis,
to the furniture in living room,
the discreet organist congregated
with pipes and vessels in dear skin.

The self-absorbed musician,
using the slipper-shod method,
hummed for definitions when inequality
burst through the whole system
in mass-execution style: Allostasis
pounded out Requiem for Glands on the ivories.

Edgy nerve endings tore up contracts
with muscles and ligaments.
Frightened fingers out on limbs
let go, and the trunk plummeted: Timbre.
Stress ricocheted within the rib cage:

A mall gunman within every mannequin,
the amydalated backbone racking up reasons.
Asteroid opioids map for an escape route.

Brace in the diaper and bracket for wardrobes,
new arrivals. Home? No one goes, not even once.

BOOK TENT BRAWL

Brawn softens between pages in a book.
Small black hands knead and knots
in muscles relax, turning fists into able
but open palms, training childhood fits
in novel fields that whisper
to hawk-eyed anger: Praxis makes . . .

When a hard bound brain builds a library
a crossroads appear with VIP seating
on Anxiety Mountain, where every tough guy
and weakling belongs: the Club for Living.
The big questions rumble by along
the expressways; some with 24-hour
wheels and some with tank treads.
Time to think about and around.

Regardless what the answer,
each king on the hill gets transported
in the same body across state lines.
Until the last breath, the gut punch remains
with the Southpaw reader who may
even practice swashbuckling with a pen.

INK ATHLETICS

Every scribbler at the poetry gym,
tumbled for nine months
in a deprivation tank before the Ta-da
onto a parquet floor.
The Epic Treadmill & Co. takes on
all feet, and barbells that wait
for tomorrow defer in homage
to yesterday dumbbells.
Young bards line up
for squat-session enjambments
or compete at pull-up allusions.

On raised platforms irony pumpers
clean and jerk for imaginary readers
while hip postmodern dance troupes
hop for the best results: Cha-cha zumba!
Going nowhere fast
upon stationary bikes,
wanna-be Shakespeares
endure but fall off
when shifting gears into prose.

Images hang from walls
for muscle assessment:
Every sonneteer reflects on one.
Old rhymers, who stretched to snap
metaphors for decades,
lie about on mats, extending
lyre wire hand ligaments,
or meditating yoga positions
with a mug for green tea iced.

Leaving the locker room for home,
a sneaker couplet figures in speech, a Homer.

AMYGDALA SONG

The strategies to hide
the meat upon meat sacrifices
clash on a small planet.
Once upon even flat terrain
barbarians stayed at home
with rituals, witnesses, and blades.

Ways through life shroud
with gods or progress
so that blood and gore
splash elsewhere.
Without land enough to absorb
each memory catalogue,
the meme systems meet,
rams aligning head and horn.

A scapegoat-common-to-all
blinding technique edges
further and further away.
The cut-throats, palm-nailers,
and drone-throwers jigsaw
the continents into dust,
into oceans, or into thin air.

Reciprocal goodwill tumbles
across deserts unless creatures
from every marching order
and programmed limbic rule
leave behind atonement day.

JEWEL FOR MARY

Oyster-consciousness praxis
cloisters from the happiness hunt
and shields from pain prevention, the mission –
The Hollywood movie version: "up the middle,"
"straight-arming" with shells bursting all around.

Prayer rugs, yoga mats, etc: great, but distract.
With no finishing line in sight,
the gods and heroes cycle around the globe
honking horns and ringing bells,
one race after another,
the tainted, accused, and martyred.

An aware mollusk-meat, in a brined bone
at the bottom during the sea changes,
gathers from dunes to turn a worry stone
into granular evidence to affirm in chant
the innocent calcium-deposited scapegoat:

One grain crafted by the tongue in a head
(that could spit or smile) rolls on a wind,
the pearl that votes with feet
for an ending to mythology.

HABITAT FOR HUMANITY

Housed in habit, the nail biter
and nose picker stretch out on the easy
waiting for the difficult surfaces,
spring offensives, a lumpy lumbar buttress.

At the convention center,
the member invests in momentum minutia
to reinforce the quirks and impulse treadmills
where embedding always trends
toward emptiness, and the breathing
patterns sprawl without purpose.

Scapegoat-ready.

Buried in thoughts not far away,
the moral improvement memeplex
plugs into any talent or untapped ability.

The practice that advises for a greater glandster
lays out goals, trophies, a honed suite
Homeo Stasis or a Juliet, protracted or shrunken,
within a more unified herd.

Silly billy or milly, the kid not butting
by recognized rules, rears by a different
humming, a tune also short on reason
and long on chorus, enough for knife and neck
to nix slaughter rites and myth for good.

BEHAVIOR BLOG

Telling a version, behavior complicates
the myth playing in Technicolor in the cranium
and the tome rolling off the tongue.

Noble prized authors, the letter carrier,
and apprentice acrobat, practice daily,
shave from imperfection a whisker
that falls to the floor, a crumpled page.

"Stillness," written by a Zen guru
and a monk, murders and pillages often.

Where, while someone suffers,
fingertips execute a meditation
on freedom and responsibility,
existential philosophers write
until the cows come home,
a cry for every body to pick up a pen.

Caveat acts, the bracketed, ellipses,
(and don't forget the contradictions),
hammering H.O.M.E., tug at sleeves
that dance above computer keys,
ghosts for maybe and not so.

DOMINOS EVERYONE?

At arm length uniform ivories
wearing mismatched buttons
stand at attention against time:
No bayonets, no bullets.

Laughable reflex opts
for flat footed bones
every moment while enduring
atmospheric pressures.

Up to waists in dobs or not,
one dot tumbles and all follow,
a grand design, perhaps.

The winners may sit-out the game
with lust-filled, yet Platonic, eyes.

Perhaps how many tiles used
determines at what length
a life lover goes on:
Talk, tick, talk, tick.

Perhaps the fancy tricks
as health topples makes for wonder
and those points count:
Hevesh5 & Kaplamino.

Even ink spots on paper warble
to hint at cognitive wobble
and collapse, an accordion,
before sight, before joints,
before lungs.

BEAMING FOR SCOTTY

Within the Contingency Temple
the contortionist quick-change-artist
and student worship at the altar
where high-priest chimeras serve up altered
pretzels, snake-skin suits, and college degrees.

Ghosts hang around familiar faces.

Sticks-in-the-mud, slow-pokes,
and one-act-ponies hunt for recent
acquaintances within stacks
of laundry, among stage scenery,
and in public libraries.

Event oceans clean up momentary beaches
where stands took place that seemed
to breach the future with substance.

Eras and epochs speed by
in ever shinier and stranger vehicles:
Mud huts, brick work, glass and steel,
and space station hook-ups,
the chain that enslaves.

Struggling attempts to conspire
with coincidence to win over shape-shifter fate.
Slapping at the eternal with the hands
and faces on clocks . . . ,

the desperate faith healer
weaves and bobs, and then on tip toe
pivots, looking for the special our,
the owner ship deed for infinity.

THE PARTING OPUS

The heavy tome titled *Resignation*
sits on the engraved desk lid
in the schoolroom for death
as Jack-in-Box prompts,
imagination and desire,
pound from the inside.

The knight-for-internal-reservations,
Paige Turner, within the new leaf catalog,
commits to breeze chapters and worse –
how to:

Pivot from the Improbable Ledge
to descend Mount Impossible;

pluck feathers from Daedalus wax;

eat with 12 apostles at the OK Corral Grill;

become one with Buddha happiness in 12 Steps;

fold away any picnic blanket;

hand down Gandhi gall and loin cloth;

lay down the walking stick
that doubles as a Spartan spear;

and study the Stoic secret hand shakes
that jitter loose grips on pens and wrinkle paper
while learning the word for no sound.

EXIT STRATEGY

an ancient and nearly forgotten art: how to navigate by the stars.

—JILL LEPORE

While the new angel slaps and flaps over shoulders,
Saint Vincent De Paul takes up the flanks
and the Salvation Army defends from the rear:
The desperation regiment,
avoiding the logo-sleepwalk,
turns to exit the corporate POW dungeon.

Savoring the honey outside in the Milky Way
any American rebels commune around space craft.
With each sock darned step by step,
a foot distances from the flooding disaster.

The pathfinder doesn't scream about fire
in the shadow cinema without puppets
stringing up by the neck.
A secession cadet points out the exit sign;
the inferno rages.
Artists reach into and pull from the wound,
and the first aid crafts under the sun
floating within the compass.

CPSIA information can be obtained
at www.ICGtesting.com
Printed in the USA
FSHW011439230620

9 781725 269873